# THE ONE WEEK MANAGER

*A Guide for Eliminating Stress in Small Business
and Work at Home Settings*

*Linda, with every best
wish!
Larry*

*7-14-21*

## LARRY LOSONCY, PH.D.

# The One Week Manager: A Guide for Eliminating Stress in Small Business and Work at Home Settings

Written by a licensed marriage and family therapist with more than 40 years of professional experience, and a lifetime of small business experience, learning from practice with his clients and advice from his peers.

Bottom line: If it is legal and ethical, do what works. This handy little book is all about what works.

**The One Week Manager:** A Guide for Eliminating Stress in Small Business and Work at Home Settings

Larry Losoncy, Ph.D.

Copyright © 2020 Larry Losoncy, Ph.D.

First Printing: October 2020

# Lawrence Losoncy Ph.D., LMFT

Dr. Losoncy (Larry) holds a master's degree in ancient and medieval philosophy, and a doctorate in the philosophy of education, which he earned by doing pioneering work in relating developmental psychology to faith development, the teaching of religion and parenting. He is an accomplished pipe organist, and has taught school at every level of education—from grades one through twelve, to college, graduate, post-graduate, adult and community education—before training as a psychotherapist. He has practiced as a clinical therapist for more than 43 years, and currently works with couples, families, and children, with a specialty in child (ages two through six) and parental development.

Larry is no stranger to stress. He was trapped in the wreckage of his family's car as a child, thrown from the bed of a pickup at 60 miles per hour as a teenager and narrowly escaped certain death in a near airplane disaster. He and his family experienced the week-long Detroit riot of 1977; and he has lived the grief of losing loved ones: siblings, parents, grandparents and friends. All of these experiences have made it easier for him to relate to others experiencing similar losses. He has worked with PTSD patients and recovering combat veterans. The common thread is stress. He worked as the Indian Child Welfare Director for a small tribe in Oklahoma for six years, participating in numerous highly emotional court cases. He is an expert in working with people suffering from the intense stress that comes from ungrieved or unfinished grief.

Larry has also been in business for himself, with experience in construction, training, inventing, sales and consulting. More importantly, over the years he has learned from many of his clients in all types of business how they handle stress: the many little things that add up to working stress-free while making a living.

# TABLE OF CONTENTS

# ONE
# ONE WEEK MANAGERS

The One Week Manager is all about managing stress in the small business setting. Stress is a reaction, both physical and emotional, to what are known as "stressors," or triggers. The most common of these in the business setting are described in the following pages, along with a variety of strategies for eliminating, avoiding, or reducing them, so that doing business is less stressful or stress free. These strategies also work very well in business-like activities: those administrative activities of everyday life such as paying bills or managing time that are necessary to maintain the household and take care of life's necessities. WORK CAN BE FUN, ENJOYABLE, PEACEFUL, FULFILLING. In the small business setting, the person in charge sets the tone and makes the difference. So, this book is for you if you manage a small business, work alone, work at home, provide the leadership in a working group or manage a smaller part of a large company.

Nearly half of all the jobs in the United States are created by small businesses, companies classed by the government as having fewer than 500 employees. Abundant and varied, there are millions of small businesses: family owned shops, restaurants, golf courses, farms, day cares, investor-owned businesses, sanitation companies, independent attorneys, private practice doctors, roofers, accountants, landscapers, architects, life coaches, home health providers, apartment managers…the list goes on. Then there are also millions more persons who are not officially in business, but whose work involves business-like activity, such as ministers, life coaches, mental and behavioral health therapists and providers, artists, writers, investors, inventors. Many people in these occupations would not even think of themselves as business managers, but they are indeed managing the business they conduct.

Managing business stress implies that business activity, even on a small scale, generates tasks and situations that could be considered stressors. Stressors are anything to which we react with a heightened state of awareness, whether that be worry, anxiety, fear, etc. Such reactions include not only an emotional, but also a physical response. Stressors, like beauty, are in the eye of the beholder. In fact, one person's stressor might be another person's cup of tea. Anyone who manages a small business operation will indeed experience stress over one thing or another, and in many cases, more stress than not. The small business operation is, at root, organized chaos.

This guide offers suggestions to eliminate or avoid some stressors, and to reduce the overall toll unavoidable stressors can take. It is intended to help you think about your situation until you devise strategies that work for you. The goal is to help you enjoy the challenge of managing without killing yourself or becoming a nervous wreck. I write this book with the realization that no two situations are the same. Having been in business most of my life—and having heard from many others who have shared some of their business wisdom with me as clients, friends or advisors—I realize that each person, in the end, needs to figure out for themselves what works best.

As a husband, father and grandfather I also am keenly aware that there are stressors in our everyday home life when we tend to the business side of life. As a therapist, my heart goes out to those single parents, and their families, for whom family life in today's world is a battle just to survive.

The **One Week Manager's** approach is to merge good business practices with good stress management to the benefit of one's self and family, as well as those employees, associates, volunteers, vendors and customers with whom you may be associated.

## Everything in Perspective

Perspective is difficult to achieve, and easy to lose. One of the first signs of the presence of stressors is the loss of perspective. Most of us already have in our minds the perfect scenario for how to be the boss, and it is not just some abstract set of ideas. The books and movies tell us all about good bosses and bad bosses. Naturally, we want to be like the good bosses on TV—cool characters with a calm disposition, a shrewd mind, and years of wisdom and excellent judgment (and, of course, success!).

Delegating responsibility is by far the recommended management style these days.

The person at the top is there to make sure everyone else is supported as they accomplish their responsibilities. When this approach is fine-tuned, the super boss should be free to watch, listen and help others in the company to keep the operation whirring at warp speed and peak efficiency.

However, the smaller the business, the more such an approach becomes unworkable, for the simple reason that there is no management staff, nobody to whom anything can be delegated! You are the boss and there is no one else to help you be the boss! So, managing by delegation becomes impossible. Forget about being a one-minute manager or a two-minute manager. Your only choice is to manage by the week.

## Managing by the week

What does it mean to manage by the week? **First** and foremost, it means that you must **prioritize**. From all the tasks needing to be completed, which ones most urgently need to be accomplished? Which duties are too important to put off, and need to be at the top of the list? Priorities are important because, in small operations, the manager must do more with less staff. It helps to establish a weekly time frame rather than a daily one, which gives you time to do those priority items, and reduces the potential stress that is generated by trying to get everything done in a shorter period of time. When, eventually, you can afford to increase your staff, you can delegate, hopefully becoming a "one-day" manager instead of a "one-week" manager.

**Second,** managing by the week means that at some points during the week **you must get the priority tasks finished.** The rest of the time you may pick away at other tasks, as the situation allows. "As the situation allows" is the key concept. The smaller the business, the more vulnerable you will be to interruptions such as phone calls, walk-ins, personal conversations and errands, and/or computer breakdowns and other equipment problems. You do not control each minute, or even most minutes of the week.

There is not a sufficient buffer between you and all the persons and happenings that can interrupt your work without warning. There is no staff to handle the various interruptions. You squeak out what work time you can for some of the most important tasks that need to be done. The rest of the time you go with the flow. You manage by the week, not by the minute.

**Third,** managing by the week means you **pick your spots for concentrated effort**.

Some moments are less vulnerable to interruption. These might be very early or very late in the day. There may be certain days in the week that are relatively quiet. Lacking enough of these moments, it may be necessary for you to simply pick a time to shut down to the rest of the world, in order to finish the work that you must finish. Put the phones on automatic, lock the front door and post reduced business hours. Close the blinds and get to work. If you work at home, put up the "Do Not Disturb" sign, and do not answer the phone. Only leave your office if it is on fire.

The manage-by-the-week approach is not particularly efficient, but when push comes to shove, it is the only approach that works without undue stress, until you can hire more people to whom you can delegate. It is based on the reality that there are limits to what a one-boss business can do. When the boss cannot get the work done, the business is history. Reality dictates the limits within which to work. That's the secret to stress-free management in small business: **stay with reality!**

No need to feel pressured, inadequate or incompetent. Start out by admitting that you are only incompetent compared to the big business manager, who has a cast of thousands. Do not make the comparison. It is not a crime to be small! It is tortuous, however, to be small but hold one's self to standards that apply to larger enterprises. The one-week manager accomplishes very few tasks on any given day. Just make sure that what gets accomplished are the vital tasks. Then go to bed, and sleep the sleep of the just.

## The whole big picture

Is it redundant to say, "the whole big picture?" Not for

the small business manager. Your job demands that you keep one eye on the daily details, and the other eye on the big picture—what is happening with the company overall. You must make decisions and give leadership from the perspective of what is best for the company, not only today, but in the long run. How will today's decisions and activities impact the rest of the company's near and distant future? That's the big picture. How well you make decisions, provide leadership and maintain perspective depends on how well you are able to keep track of the big things, while attending to the small things. Understanding the whole big picture is the art and discipline of paying attention to details, while keeping perspective. This is nearly impossible unless you are in reasonably good shape, of sound mind, and emotionally stable. In other words, **you need to have a life.** That is where the "whole" comes into play.

The big picture has to do with the company you manage. The whole picture has to do with your life. Managers who are nervous wrecks really are not very good for their companies. The only way to not be a nervous wreck is to get a life. It's that simple. The ability to have a life and be a business manager, however, does not come easy in today's business climate. We are at a time of intense productivity and competition. Much to everyone's amazement, we are discovering that it takes a great deal of time to be technologically efficient.

At the dawn of the computer age, we were told that humans could be replaced by technology. Automation would replace our labor. Computers would reduce the time needed for data management, shrinking computation from hours to seconds. Humans could rest their backs and their minds. The problem would be how to manage all our extra leisure time. What happened, instead, is that technology and computers have simply allowed us humans to become more productive. Now that we have greater capacity to accomplish more, we are driven to do so. The law of "produce or perish" remains in effect. Managers feel this crunch. The demand is for more of our hours at work, not less. Everything has sped up!

It has become ever more difficult for managers to keep track of both the big picture and the whole picture. They must manage with perspective for the sake of not only their employees and their company, but also themselves. Policies reflect the policymaker's point of view. **Goofy managers make work a living hell for their workers.**

The first and best way to reduce stress in the workplace is to reduce your own stress. The best way to ensure you're coming to work stress free is to have a life and purpose beyond your job. Here is the simple one-question test: **When your workday is finished, can you hardly wait to go home, share life with people you love, and engage in meaningful activities that you enjoy?** It is good for you, your family and your company that you have a life beyond your work. When you are gathered unto your final reward, do you really want your tombstone to read: "Here lies a business manager who gave all for the cause?" If so, you are missing the whole picture. Both the company and your workers could pay the price. And you could need that tombstone much quicker than expected!

## Know Thyself.

Socrates said it first and best, when he admonished us to "know thyself." It is a good starting point in the search for wisdom. Socrates could spend all night standing still, just thinking. He was famous for what we in this day and age would call inner peace, or composure. He was a very low stress person. He was sentenced to death because he had come to the conclusion—and was teaching the Greeks—that there could not be many gods, as the Greeks believed, but only one God, an un-caused first cause of all things. He could easily have fled and escaped the death penalty, a common practice for those sentenced to death in the Greek city states. Instead he chose to drink hemlock as a witness to his convictions. He calmly dialogued with his closest friends as he prepared to die. His reaction to this most stressful of all events stands as an historic example of being in touch with one's self

Business managers are not called upon to die for their convictions, thank goodness! But the first and most important step in stress management, knowing one's self, leads to inner peace and direction.

**What are your frustration points?**

**What are your strengths and weaknesses?**

**What do you most enjoy among your many work tasks; and what do you least enjoy?**

**At what aspects of your job are you the least efficient?**

What aspects of your job take you longer than they should? For example:

**Do you dread bookkeeping and filing?**

**Do you hate paying bills?**

**Do you dislike preparing invoices and reports?**

**Does keeping records on your employees prove painful?**

**Do you dread being direct with employees and associates in doing performance reviews?**

**Do you find it difficult to give orders and directives or redirection?**

**Is it difficult for you to leave the office at night with important work unfinished?**

Based upon your strengths, what aspects of your job do you perform most efficiently?

**What do you accomplish rapidly?**

**What do you enjoy the most?**

**What gives you the most satisfaction?**

A note of caution: sometimes we are not very good at the tasks we most enjoy. Sometimes we are very good at the tasks we least enjoy. In the same vein, sometimes we are quickest at the things we do worst, and slowest at the things we do best. Knowing ourselves includes a careful self-analysis of how well we use our time, and the reasons why we take longer at some tasks and less time at others. Knowing what makes us tick as business managers yields the starting point for developing strategies to get the most accomplished in the least amount of time, and with the least amount of stress. But figuring it all out is not necessarily a quick process. It takes a lifetime to know and accept ourselves.

The overall strategy for minimizing stress is to do the things at which you are best and quickest, and enjoy the most. Get others, to the extent possible, to do the tasks at which you are not quick or particularly efficient, or that you dislike the most. Be sure, if you delegate these tasks to employees, that you do not saddle an employee with a task he or she is not good at, not quick at, or happens to dislike doing. Consider outsourcing. Somebody out there must like doing what you do not like doing.

There is no rocket science in this approach. We all feel better when we accomplish something successfully. Remember the old adage, **"success breeds success."**

## Stay current and do your research

Research is an important part of knowing one's self and developing perspective. "Oh sure," you might reply. "I'll do that in all the spare time I do not have!" Therein lies a trap, because staying current and doing research are not activities reserved for those managers who are not constantly busy. Most, if not all managers, are constantly busy. Small business managers are often much too busy. Often, the temptation is to consider staying current with the profession or industry as something that happens automatically.

It is also often tempting to consider doing research relating to product, services and costs of doing business as not necessary and/or not possible. Try telling that to the folks raising catfish, or the manager who plans to purchase a faster printing press for the county newspaper! Try telling the family farmer that it is not necessary to watch market prices, continually research crop market trends and stay abreast of recommended best practices for maximum yields and environmental sustainability. While it may seem nerve-wracking to do research, it ought to be far more nerve-wracking not to do so! And, indeed, that is the case. Research helps managers stay current. For some, **belonging to a professional organization** is the best way to keep abreast of innovations and obtain advice from others. **Networking** is another way. Stay current on important business issues, such as:

- tax codes
- safety and environmental regulations
- reporting requirements
- new competition
- customer satisfaction
- changes in interest rates
- marketing trends
- new ideas for product improvements

The smaller the business, the easier it is to stay current and do research. This is due, in part, to the informality that you might not find in a larger business. That informality can be a shortcut to gaining insight. For example: look around your world for the person who does what you do exceptionally well. This might be the local legend, the business leader everyone agrees is the best. Reach out to this person for an informational interview about what they have learned over the years that you should know about. Perhaps they know about a website with valuable information, saving you hours of internet searching. Perhaps they go about things in some different way that works for them—and could work for you.

The sincerest form of flattery is imitation. The second most sincere form of flattery is to seek a reputable businessperson's opinion about a specified problem, trend or trade practice. What is the secret of their success? Even better, if such persons are retired, what do they have to share in retrospect? The number one reason why successful people do not share their secrets is because they are not asked. The number one reason they are not asked is because their peers do not notice and/or study what they do.

Another shortcut to market research is to ask one person every day what they know about your product or services. Then ask them for advice. Write it down. Make sure you ask a different person every day. At the end of each month read what you have written. Yet another shortcut: at the end of every phone conversation with your customers or clients, ask them if they have any advice for your business, and jot down notes. It's not that you need to do everything or anything that you are advised to do. Rather, those bits and pieces of replies will paint a picture of what people think of your product and services—and of you. Their impressions tell you what kind of image you portray, if any. It will set you to thinking. It is information that does not cost anything, and only takes a few minutes each day to gather. It gets you listening, observing, thinking and concentrating about what can be done to improve.

There are four sets of people from whom feedback is important:

- your peers
- your customers
- your employees
- the public at large

Except for occasional complaints, you will get almost no feedback unless you ask. Listen and thank these persons for their comments.

That is how to stay current and do research in the world of small business. Most surprisingly, when you do these simple things you will discover yourself listening to the news more intently, reading newspapers and newsletter more thoughtfully, and waking up with new ideas about how to improve, protect or modify your business plans and practices. And you won't be stressed out, wondering what potentially harmful developments are happening that you don't know about. In due time, you will become the legend!

**Become a legend in your field by listening to ideas and feedback from your peers, customers, employees and the public at large. They will only tell you what they**

**think if you ask them. So, ask them!!**

How does listening to others and doing research help us get to know ourselves better? Because it helps us get rid of blind sides. It has long been an axiom of psychological and personality theory that we have four selves, as it were. These are:

- the person I think I am
- the person others think I am
- the person I think others think I am
- the person I really am

Listening and researching helps to get rid of blind sides, and discover the real me. If I become a legend in my own mind, I will never know myself. A researcher named Jahari put it this way: it is as though each of us have four windows about self. There is the **open window:** the part of myself I share with others. I see that part of myself and so do they. There is the **hidden window**: I see that part of myself but keep it hidden from others. There is the **blind side** of myself that others see but I do not. There is the **dark side** which neither I nor others see. To truly gain perspective the blind side needs to get smaller and smaller as I stop denying and defending against what I need—but do not want—to hear. To hear the truth from others and build genuine trust, the hidden side also needs to go. The open window is the road to perspective that allows us to consider the whole big picture: self, others, the good of the company and a road to the future.

# TWO
# TIPS, TRICKS, NUTS, and BOLTS OF
# STRESS MANAGEMENT

## What Does a Manager Actually Manage?

Just in case you happen to believe that working outdoors and having your own one-person business is a wonderful life, ask the first lawn-care person you meet how stress-free the business is. He or she will likely tell you it is completely stress-free when the weather is good, mowing is on schedule, customer payments are current, bills are paid and the equipment is in good working order. In all other circumstances, even the "lucky" person you notice out there mowing a lawn is neither carefree, nor without plenty of stressful triggers with which to contend.

This chapter and the next present ideas and approaches for managing with a minimum of stressors. Facing, rather than ignoring, problems is always the better way. Denial goes nowhere. Use the ideas that work for you, occasionally utilizing new approaches you come across. Remember the rule of thumb for small business management: **do what works.**

## Quit Trying to Manage People

A play on words? No, indeed! We use the term "manage people" too lightly, but so frequently that managers often believe they do manage people. What in fact do we actually manage?

- **Use of time**
- **Data**
- **Schedules**
- **Processes, such as transport, inventory, quality control, research, reporting, performance reviews**
- **Finances**
- **Pensions, retirement plans, resources**
- **Planning**

Managers who believe that they manage people will experience a very large amount of stress. They will also trigger stress in the persons they try to manage. Why is this?

Managing people contradicts reality. The only person anyone can manage is one's own self. Managers need to manage themselves. When they try to manage others, the reaction is always the same: each person still decides what to think, how to feel and how to behave. When the orders are not agreeable, the person will become resentful. The reaction will be roughly the same as the reaction we all have when we are told up is down or first is second or good is bad: it does not compute

So, even if managers believe that they are managing people, what they are actually doing is providing coordination and leadership for the behaviors and work of the people over whom they have authority. Like the manager of a professional sports team, the manager does not play the game, only the players play the game. The manager develops the game plan and coaches the players on how best to achieve the game plan.

Bottom line: managers do not manage people. If you, as a manager, find yourself stressed and worrying, think about this: whose problems are you taking on as your responsibility? Each person under you is responsible for managing themselves. Your job is to let them do that and encourage them to do that. You should be the least worried person because all of "your people" are managing themselves. This style of management requires specific skills. It is not benign neglect. Coaching and practice can help you quickly acquire (or sharpen) these skills, if you are not already using them.

## Assess and Communicate Responsibilities

First and foremost, among these specific skills is the ability to accurately and consistently assess and communicate who is responsible for what. Exactly how much of this project, job, piece of work or problem is your responsibility, and how much is theirs? How much belongs to you, and how much belongs to them, individually? You can only take care of the part that belongs to you. You must expect that they will take care of their part. The ability to manage in this fashion is both art and science. It begins with a firm and clear point of view. Managers do not manage people. They provide leadership for people to manage themselves. **You do not own the people who work for you.**

## Nothing Is Ever Enough: Know When to Quit

We have all heard the refrain, "My work is never done." Usually, the person uttering this phrase means to say that there is more work to do than time in the day for doing it. Most people who hear such a remark take it as a sign of dedication. The business coach hearing such a sentiment, however, makes a mental note: here is a person on a collision course with burnout—unless they learn the skill of knowing when to quit. Reflect for a moment on the stress you feel when a task must be left unfinished. Even more to the point, imagine that the task did not get finished in the specific amount of time that you knew was sufficient. When the amount of time is reasonable, but the job still isn't finished, we all know something went wrong.

We stress when something goes wrong. We stress when we miss a reasonable goal and fall short of achievable standards. We stress when the schedule breaks down, especially when it breaks down for reasons of carelessness or poor planning or lack of proper effort. That is how we are programmed to operate. We blame ourselves, and experience a sense of failure. Small business managers, by contrast, ride herd over tasks that seemingly never end. There is rarely enough time in the day to do everything that needs doing. Time gets allocated to do **some** of this and some of that, such as

- make some of the return phone calls
- follow up on some customer satisfaction inquiries
- visit with some of the employees or service contractors
- read some of the more important trade information
- do or inspect some work on the equipment

By definition, if a small business must operate with a shortage of personnel and surplus of multi-tasking, not everything will get done at once, or on time. Therein lies the stress trap: human nature kicks in, and the manager begins to feel the frustration.

**The first instinct is to work longer, start earlier, stay later and try harder.**

**Then comes self-doubt: Am I doing my best? Will we make it?**

**Finally, the slogans: time is money, only losers quit, suck it up, how bad do you want this?**

Something inside most of us wants to believe that if we work hard enough and stay with it, the day will come when everything does get done, and we can revert back to normal hours and a sensible work schedule. The small business manager must fight this thought, and needs to encourage employees to fight it as well. As a manager, a key skill is the ability to say, in so many words, "If we work hard all day, not everything will get done; only what we are able to do will get done, and the rest will be waiting for us tomorrow."

## Define Success in Terms of What Is Achievable

It is unrealistic to define success as all or nothing. Emphasize to yourself, as well as to those around you, how the pieces, when taken together, will add up to the whole. Articulate this every single day. Make charts. Put up reminders and slogans that emphasize what is realistic. This way, you will counter the instincts we all have about wanting to complete the job, rather than walking away when the time is up.

Setting realistic daily goals and framing for everyone how the pieces make up the whole, is the leader's responsibility. "Less is more" might not fit what motivational speakers preach about going all-out and striving for success no matter the cost. In the world of small business, the problem is not always lack of effort. In some cases, the problem can be **too much effort.** Too much effort for too long leads to frustration, and frustration leads to burnout. Yes, of course, success is important for small business. But the challenge is to have staying power and to accurately define success. You and those who work with you need to be there and be in good shape when success happens.

**Do what we can today. The rest will be there tomorrow.**

## A Little Humor Goes a Long Way

It is said that the reason we laugh at something funny is because we hear the truth in it. Comedy, in a way, is the most serious of all discourse!

### There is humor based on the obvious.

"I have never been accused of being my mother's brightest son."

"Your elevator does not go all the way to the top."

"I said, for some reason people do not seem to like me, you fathead. Didn't you hear me the first time?"

"No, I have never belonged to any organized party. I have been a Democrat all my life." (Will Rogers)

Minister, after weaving down main street in his car and being stopped by the town constable:

"Officer, I was drinking water out of that bottle."

Officer: "Reverend, that is wine."

Minister: "Alleluia, He's done it again!"

### There is humor in deliberate misuse of language or logic.

"Don't ever misunderestimate me." (George W. Bush)

"You can fool some of the people all of the time. Those are the ones you want to concentrate on." (George W. Bush)

"What makes for a great team is 80 percent player talent

and 60 percent managerial genius." (Casey Stengel)

Weather forecast: "Due to a deepening tropical seclusion we can expect intense scottered thundershatters. It may rain hail-sized golf balls."

"When you come to a fork in the road, take it." (Yogi Berra)

Question: "Should I do this or do that?" Answer: "Yes"

**There is humor based on exaggeration.**

Doctor: "That wart on your nose needs to come off, it could lead to big trouble."

Patient: "Could I have a second opinion, do you mind?"

Doctor: "Heck no, it's ugly too."

"The fog is so thick; the continent is cut off from England"

"I am so fast; I get ahead of my shadow and beat it to second base."

**There is humor based on false compliments and double messages.**

"You, sir, are a brave man. Not everybody has the courage to whine and whimper in public."

"Those who are all wrapped up in themselves come in small packages." (Benjamin Franklin)

"You must be a big wheel because you keep going in circles." (Benjamin Franklin)

"Anthony Eden is like a ripe banana: all full of black spots on the outside and squishy on on the inside." (Winston Churchill)

Lady Astor to Winston Churchill: "If I were married to you, I would be tempted to put poison in your tea." Churchill: "If I were married to you, I would drink it."

**There is humor which uses stories to make the point.**

A painter went after the contract to paint the church. He planned to siphon off some of the paint and sell it on the side. The plan worked well: he got the contract to paint the church, inside and out. He kept thinning the paint and selling off buckets of good paint. Nobody noticed that he was getting rich. But one day a huge dark cloud formed over the church. It began to rain, inside and outside of the church, until every last drop of new paint had been washed away. Then the cloud parted and a bright golden beam of light shined down from the cloud and it said: "Repaint, repaint. Go and thin no more!"

Humor goes a long way towards defusing tension and stress. Use it liberally in the workplace. When all else fails, say something funny. And oh yes, make sure that the humor is appropriate. Don't be telling seemingly funny death stories at wakes and don't make stupid boss jokes when your vice president is trying to give you advice about improving your performance! Above all, never ever use sarcasm. Sarcasm, while funny, also hurts, and is never appropriate.

**Humor is supposed to help us laugh, not hurt our feelings.**

# THREE
# MORE NUTS AND BOLTS

## What About Multi-Tasking?

It would be a fair guess that almost all of the managers and owners of very small businesses have to engage in multi-tasking every day. There are two types of multi-tasking: enjoyable, and horrible. It is most likely that one will either love multi-tasking or hate it. While it is stressful no matter what, multi-tasking is even more anxiety-inducing for those who hate it. Those who don't hate it tend to derive a certain degree of satisfaction from "conquering" the challenge, proving to themselves that they can handle the situation when the chips are down, and it is do or die. Those who hate it often have difficulty concentrating and staying focused.

Try this simple layman's test (answer yes or no):

**Do you enjoy, and do reasonably well, while doing such things as watching TV and reading something light at the same time?**

**Are you able to converse while doing some other task at the same time?**

**Can you follow two lines of thought at the same time without getting a headache?**

If you answered yes to these questions, there is no reason you cannot handle—or even learn to enjoy—multi-tasking, with little to no anxiety. The point is to achieve a minimum of stress and a maximum amount of satisfaction from multi-tasking. If your answer to any of these three questions was "no", multi-tasking must be approached slowly and carefully. It will likely cause you fits if you try to rush; and employees who aren't prone to multi-tasking will want to quit if they are pressured to do so. If you or any of your employees have serious problems with this issue, it might be advisable to consider outsourcing some of the tasks involved, reviewing and redistributing tasks and responsibilities, or rotating some of the most stressful tasks. Ignoring this sort of stress is an open invitation to burnout: yours, or that of those who may work for you.

It is said that Napoleon Bonaparte would dictate letters 12 at a time, using 12 secretaries. He would move from one secretary to the next, remembering where he had left off with each letter and continuing each dictation accurately, as he made the rounds from one secretary to the next. That is a classic example of multi-tasking. We should all be so gifted! Unlike fighting a war, small business challenges are not very dramatic, but they can be very stressful.

We find ourselves trying to sort mail and answer a phone call simultaneously. We try to finish something on the computer, while jotting down important things to remember to do next, tasks that we forgot to jot down before we got started on the day's list of to do's. Often, we find ourselves of necessity stopping with a task half-finished because something more important, such as speaking with a distressed employee or customer, has come up. Then, we must return to the first task to get it finished and hope to pick up the train of thought.

## Three Secrets of Managing Multi-Tasking

There is never enough time to take a break because the work of managing is never finished. That is where the three secrets for managing the stress of multi-tasking come into play. They are:

**Maintain good order.**

**Turn frustration into satisfaction.**

**Manage the use of time.**

### Maintain Good Order

The most common casualty of the inevitable stop-and-go work pace is filing. It is so easy to pile up things that need to be filed. Those piles grow almost as if by magic. Filing is the first key for those wishing to achieve good order. **Never**

**let a day go by without finishing the filing.** Filing is the secret to being able to find things! Spending time looking around for information, letters, bills, receipts and messages is probably the number one cause of frustration in the small business management arena. Therein lies the second key to heading off frustration: turn frustration into satisfaction.

## Turn Frustration into Satisfaction

Satisfaction makes a joy out of what otherwise would be a budding nightmare. Good order begins with finding things. Finding things begins with putting them where they belong. Putting them where they belong means attention to filing, every day, perhaps every few hours. The manager's work is not dramatic or earth shaking most of the time. In fact, it can be so ordinary that the lack of challenge itself becomes a road to burnout. The secret is always the same: view the tasks as satisfying instead of boring. If this approach means taking more time, then so be it. Better to work longer and get the job done right, than to hurry and work in a constant state of uproar, frustration, disorganization and low-grade chaos, always trying to do two or three things at the same time.

## Manage Your Time

Schedule breaks if you ever want them to happen! The road to patience runs right through managing a small business. It starts with reflecting on what strategies will be most effective for handling multi-tasking. No matter your approach, there are fundamentals that will always help. These include organizing the daily activities, scheduling them and sticking to the schedule as much as is practical. For a schedule to make sense day after day, certain simple components come into play:

- an organized approach to filing
- organizing and prioritizing the day's tasks
- keeping track of what needs to be done tomorrow
- carefully attending to messages
- keeping routine and clear notes in the date book, and accurately posting deadlines
- taking frequent short breaks instead of waiting for a "better time" to take a break.

So, multi-tasking in the small business setting is impossible to avoid; but it can be turned into a plus by maintaining good order, turning frustration into satisfaction and managing time wisely. Make lemonade out of lemons.

## Local Standard Time

Managing time wisely begins with learning how to tell time when the time is local standard time (LST). Many small businesses are conducted with local employees, customers and vendors. Local standard time is how the people around you tell time. When nobody in town comes to work until 9:15 a.m., that means starting time according to LST is 9:15 a.m. You can get your blood pressure up 20 points trying to make your people arrive at 9 a.m. sharp, when they constantly show up at 9:15; or, you will find yourself firing them.

The smaller the business, the more likely it runs

according to LST. The smallest of businesses, office at home, is the most influenced. That is because households always run on LST. There is a right time for meals, a right time for shopping, a right time for everything. The correct hours for working at your small business in home are easily determined: they are those hours during which no one else in your home interrupts you with important matters that need taking care of immediately.

Small businesses outside of the home are also influenced by LST, because those who work for you and with you are very close to home. They might have children, so the beginning and end of the school day is LST. Everything else gets organized around getting their children to and from school. Their household routines may dictate that they go home for lunch with a partner, or look in on an elderly parent. The closer to home, the stronger the pull; and the more important it becomes for employees and helpers to integrate work into the rest of their schedule, helping businesses that run on Local Standard Time to thrive.

As a manager your choice is to fight LST or go with the flow. Those who fight it battle in vain, and needlessly create stress for themselves. Those who honor it will encounter loyalty and appreciation—and far less stress! Here is how to honor LST:

- Avoid local sales calls the day before a holiday.
- Give your people time off when the whole town is cleaning up after a storm or a parade.
- Do not schedule overtime on Wednesday nights if

your people have Church on Wednesdays.

- Do your own overtime work very early in the morning, before anyone else wakes up, while
- there is still peace and quiet across the world.
- Thursdays are better than Fridays to ask your people to work late, because Fridays are
- the start of weekend madness. Perhaps people could start early and work late on Thursdays, in order to end their work week at noon on Fridays.

Managing time is a different concept than controlling time. Nobody controls time, although many stressed- and burned-out managers suffer from the illusion that they do. Recognize that there are only five kinds of time over which you have an influence:

- **Startin' time**
- **Quittin' time**
- **Overtime**
- **Halftime**
- **Vacation time**

When you set these times in accordance with LST, your employees and helpers will be more punctual. They will also go home on time. They will let you know when overtime will work well for them. And they will use the time they have for working with you to maximum efficiency. **Productivity goes up when everyone involved knows how to tell time. And you will sleep much better!** Why is this? It is because humans bring to their tasks something computers do not: a brain.

Unlike computers, that brain begins to malfunction with constant use. Humans are subject to fatigue. Humans are subject to burnout. Tired humans have more accidents, become less efficient, make mistakes, get discouraged and are apt to quit the company if they are overworked long enough. In other words: time out is important. Statistically, American workers are among the most productive in the world. That's good—and bad. Overworking is an easy trap to fall into. Start with good management of your own time-outs, then make sure your people are also using time-outs wisely.

## Breaks

The right number of breaks is exactly however many are needed. This varies from day to day, and task to task. Intense computer work demands breaks geared to rest the eyes. Manual labor calls for breaks to rest the back. It would be wise to schedule several mandatory breaks throughout the day, including lunch, while also encouraging impromptu breaks, as needed. Force yourself to use these breaks, and insist that your workers do the same.

## Quitting Time

Many of us have worked for the boss who had no quitting time for him or herself. He or she would work until they became too tired to move or even see straight. These were the worst kind of boss because they imposed their quitting time standard on those whom they managed. The job never ended. Leaving work at the end of the workday was viewed as betrayal.

Start with yourself. "A good manager goes home when the day is done." Say that over and over until it becomes your mantra. The implication, of course, is that a good manager organizes the work to be done in a realistic manner. When is your workday done? When does your workday begin? What is a realistic amount of work to be accomplished within that time frame? When your quitting time rolls around, the thing to do is **go home.** Your work will be waiting for you when you come back. The world does not hinge on your doing several extra hours of work every day. But your life outside of work might well hinge on having you there, instead of working overtime. Have you ever heard of anyone on their death bed saying "Gee, I wish I could work another day?"

When you have six good hours to work on a given day, schedule six hours of work for yourself, not seven or eight or nine! Six hours might be par for the course, given time out for breaks and lunch and interruptions. Your first responsibility when it comes to time management is getting the most out of the time available. That begins with recognizing how much time is actually available, first for yourself, and then for your workers. Productivity can be measured by how well that time is used. The manager who is frequently working overtime is not managing well. The employees who are frequently asked to work overtime are being mismanaged. Hours that should otherwise be spent on your personal life, or the personal lives of your employees, are being occupied by the company. This is a recipe for trouble, and an indication of serious mismanagement.

## Leaves and Vacations

The current trend for many people is to skip their vacations, cut trips short, or take work with them when they travel. This goes right along with sleep deprivation, something that has become a national epidemic. Add overtime work to this picture and what you will get is fatigue, stress, health problems, burnout and rising employee turnover rates. If you, as the manger or self-employed person, follow this recipe you will discover that work is no longer satisfying. In the end, you are likely also to discover that you can't beat the odds—you, too, will end up stressed, fatigued and battling health problems before retirement age.

The moral of the story is that all work and no play truly does make Jack a dull boy, and Jill a dull girl. So, take your breaks, go home and have a life when the workday is finished and enjoy those vacations! Many things have changed in the world of business and economics. But human nature has not changed. None of us are computers.

**Do not act like you are a computer, and do not allow workers to act like they are computers.**

# FOUR
# MENTAL ASPECTS OF MANAGING
# BUSINESS STRESS

———— ⚬❧⚬ ————

STRESS IS A BUMMER: NOT GOOD FOR ONE'S HEALTH, NOT GOOD FOR RELATING AND COMMUNICATING, DEFINITELY NOT GOOD FOR BUSINESS MANAGERS AND THOSE WHOSE WORK THEY MANAGE. OTHER FEATURES OF STRESS INCLUDE WORRY, ANXIETY, HIGH BLOOD PRESSURE AND A FEELING OF UNEASE; ALL OF WHICH MAKE ONE HARD TO LIVE WITH.

The business manager is well advised to learn effective way of preventing unnecessary stress, while managing the stress that cannot be totally avoided. Managers of small work forces will find this to be a critical factor in employee retention. The one-person business manager will find stress management to be of enormous benefit for maintaining sanity, as well as balancing home life with business endeavors. What follows is a partial list of mental stress mitigation techniques and practices related to business and business-like activities.

## Out of Sight, Out of Mind

When you are not working, quit thinking about work. Close down the workday when it is over. Put everything away, finish the filing, close the drawers, lock the security files and make notes about what to remember to do on the next business day. When you leave the work area, make sure your mind is also closed to the business. Except for emergencies, do not take work out of the office.

## Leave Work Behind When You Vacation

**"Vacation"** includes weekend getaways, days off, trips with the family, vacations, holidays and afternoons off. Enjoy your time off, and make sure your employees enjoy their time off. Don't phone in for messages, or accept calls. Don't take laptops on trips in an attempt to work while you aren't working. Get a life that is not business, and enjoy it.

## Don't Think About Work When You Try to Sleep

Thinking about work when you should be falling asleep is called worry, a big No-No in the world of stress management. If thoughts about the business break through when you are trying to sleep, get out of bed, leave the bedroom, have a good worry (maybe even jot down a few key thoughts) then once it is out of your system, go back to bed.

## What Happens At Work Stays At Work

Don't be talking shop when you aren't at the shop. Get a life and live it when you aren't at work. Have a hobby. Go fishing. Play golf. Jog. Play tennis. Go swimming. Play cards. Have fun.

## Worry on Purpose, and on Schedule, Then Let it Be

This is called venting and detachment. What will happen will happen. Worrying won't change anything. Ask yourself what would happen to the business if you died in the very near future. If the business would die with you, it is time to arrange for succession because you are going to die sooner or later. If the business is organized to survive your death or retirement, use that fact as reason enough to quit treating the business as though it were life and death.

## Talk Your Concerns and Problems Over With a Friend

"You can't see the forest for the trees" is a useful adage. Talking out problems is a big stress reliever. Sometimes a different perspective provided by a trusty friend will help us see how to navigate problems. If you are lucky that person will be a partner or business associate. Think about using a business coach. Perhaps your spouse fits the bill. Perhaps there is a friend or a trustworthy retiree who is a good listener. If you cannot think of anybody with whom to talk, you do have something to worry about.

## Confer regularly with Your Board of Directors

If you do not have a working Board, take steps to develop one, even if only an advisory Board. Your Board helps with shaping policy, and will be of enormous assistance, so long as its directors know the business, and believe in what you are doing.

## Exercise and Live Well

There is more to preventing and managing the stress of work than only these mental steps. Proper exercise, proper rest, proper sleep and good nutrition are also essential. For example, drinking soda pop and eating candy will not relieve work stress, it will only make you fat, hyperactive and/or drowsy. And mental discipline is wasted if you operate on habitual sleep deprivation. Fatigue is an open invitation to stress. Still, all the aerobic exercise, sleep and good nutritional meals will not help against stress if you approach your business responsibilities with sloppy mental habits. Staying on top of the business demands both good habits that foster health and relaxation, and good mental discipline. It is truly tragic to waste a good mind. Stress will do that to the undisciplined manager. Since your mind is the only one you have, better to take care of it by developing healthy routines to prevent and counter stress.

## Decompress Between Work and Home

Leave home at home, and leave work at work: standard advice for business managers. There are two reasons for this advice. **First**, it is good to put work out of mind, then come back to it fresh the next day, or after the weekend. Those who think about their work while outside of the workplace are prone to worry. Worry quickly leads to anxiety, and potentially, to burnout. Eventually, you may dread, or even hate, the thought of going to work. It is good for the manager—not to mention the business and employees—when he or she is off the job outside of the office.

**Second**, if the manager does not leave work at work, some of the worry, stress and problem-solving that goes on at work will creep into his or her home. That, in turn, allows the manager's work and responsibilities to move in with the family. Even for managers who live alone, and/or do not have a family, it is not good to routinely bring work home, or allow it to come home mentally.

Those who **work from home** need to develop routines that keep their work in the workplace, and prevent it from pervading the entire home and living space. This is challenging, but not by any means impossible. Start, of course, by closing down the day's tasks, putting things away, closing the files, locking up anything that needs to be secured, then closing and securing the office or workplace. That ends work physically, but it also helps to close out the workday mentally.

Those who **work away from home** might consider engaging in a short activity between work- and home-life. This could be a short walk, a few minutes in the park, a drive home listening to music or an audiobook or podcast that is neither work nor home related. For those who plunge directly into traffic, it would be advisable to take a walk once you arrive home, even before going into the house.

The same principles of keeping work at work, and home at home, apply when you leave home to go to work. Read the morning paper, take a walk, look at the flowers, have some coffee between home and work. Do something that is neither home- nor office-related as a way of leaving home behind before entering your office or workspace.

Remember, the best way to manage stress is to not have any in the first place. By leaving stressful matters behind, it is possible to go to either your workplace, or your home, with a "clean slate," instead of bringing the stress of one with you to the other. By emphasizing that you go back and forth between two worlds, as it were, you create the benefit of relief when it is needed. You allow yourself to participate with full attention wherever you are, without being bogged down by extra concerns from wherever you were. Living in the now is not something reserved for people in recovery, but something that is good for everyone.

# FIVE
# SELF DISCIPLINE: GOOD HABITS THAT HELP

## The three great temptations

Stress, especially ongoing stress, creates in most of us a craving for relief. This makes perfectly good sense in light of our survival instincts. The human instinct is to fight or flee in the face of danger. Prolonged stress registers as danger. We instinctively want to either conquer or escape the stressful situation. The results for those who are not careful and disciplined are the three great temptations:

- **Eat for relief.**
- **Skip proper exercise.**

- **Deprive the body of sleep.**

**Eating for relief** usually takes the form of turning to junk food, snacks washed down with soft drinks, and sweets in order to compensate for suffering. This, in turn, makes folks less hungry at mealtime. Instead of eating three nutritious means each day, those who eat for relief end up skipping meals here and there. Then, when hunger strikes, they overeat. Before long they suffer from heartburn, and notice that they have gained weight even though they are eating fewer than three meals per day.

**Skipping proper exercise** is the daily temptation for small business managers because the work is never finished. Managers often go to work early in the morning (there goes the morning run) and stay late (there goes the evening workout). Those who have been loading up on junk food experience profound changes in their sugar levels, leaving them feeling exhausted and, like worn out horses, just wanting to go home.

**Sleep deprivation** sets in as a result of irregular eating and lack of exercise. Snacks in the middle of the night, mood swings and muscle aches from too much sitting and not enough working out combine with worries about work. Sleep deprivation is a natural consequence for those who succumb to the first two temptations.

Those who rely on willpower to resist the three great temptations will fall victim just as surely as day follows night. If willpower were the answer there would be no one struggling with the problems being described. Put it another way: **"Good resolutions don't cut it."** The secret lies in scheduling. When you organize each day's schedule, consider more than simply what time you will begin and end work, and what tasks you will address. Schedule into your day the time of each meal (at least fifteen minutes to enjoy your food), and the time during which you will exercise. Also schedule in the exact time by which you will be in bed, giving yourself a solid eight hours to sleep. That means, of course, there will be only so much time for work, family and personal matters.

To those who cry out that there is not sufficient time in the day for all of these things, the answer is always the same: do not schedule your rest, nutrition or other time for well-being out of any day. Do not schedule those who share life with you out of any day. It truly is not a matter of willpower, but a matter of time management.

The business manager will never have enough time. Time is in short supply. As a manager you already know the importance of using well scarce resources, planning around the shortages and getting others to "work smart." Apply those same understandings to your own schedule, and follow it! It is not a matter of willpower, but a matter of organization, and the discipline to stick to the schedule. Discipline is not willpower, but a combination of planning, good habits and perseverance.

**Today is the tomorrow you worried about yesterday**

## Pencils Save Stress

A pencil could save stress? Ridiculous, right? Not so.

What are the most frustrating things that happen to business managers?

- **Losing information**
- **Not being able to find information**
- **Getting the information wrong**

Finding missing information sometimes takes more minutes, or even hours, than the phone call, email or return letter for which the information is needed. Information retrieval can be no better than the process of receiving and storing the information in the first place. A little bit of lost information here, a lost number there, a zip code written down incorrectly and the manager is ready to breathe fire. The tinier the details tripping us up the greater the frustration over wasting time.

Here is a simple suggestion: get a notepad and pencil. Place them next to your telephone and handy to your computer and use them for every single message you receive each day. Imagine that, a pencil to prevent stress! In this age of advanced technology, one communication problem persists: we need to hear or read messages accurately, and record information from those communications accurately. Given the many times every day that messages need to be returned, you as the manager can make your day easier by carefully writing down the name, number and time of each message you receive, along with what you can do to respond.

The list with the basic information then becomes a guide for tasks to be done; call the person back, email that person, send a letter, pay a bill, check an invoice. It's all there in a few words and numbers. Just be careful that those few words and numbers are accurate. They won't be accurate if you rush. There is a difference between jotting down and carefully recording information. Spend ten extra seconds carefully recording the information with each message, and you will save literally hundreds of minutes every month trying to correct mistakes. As an extra bonus, your frustration level will also drop.

When your workday is finished, save the pages you have used to record messages and pending tasks. That is part of your work order for the next day, as well as your work log. Glance over it the next time you start a workday. Store these sheets in bundles by the month. They become a backup source for reports and information when you forget to record an important number or email address that you have used in the past.

There is another value in using that pencil when you are taking a call or reading an email: it will help you to focus so that you get the full impact of the message the first time. It is so easy to get distracted and lose focus when taking a call or reading a message. The pencil is tangible. We hold it, feel it, gnaw on it and make it move when we write. It keeps us centered for a few brief seconds—just long enough to make sure that we have heard correctly and written accurately. Also, very important: remember to read back to the other party the numbers and letters you write down, double-checking the information you have recorded.

The business manager's work life is a bundle of little things needing constant and careful attention. Messages are little things. The phone numbers and internet addresses in those messages are even smaller. But it is of little things that frustration is borne, and colossal losses of time are wrought. The human fuse finally blows when enough of those little things need straightening out. Be off on the timing of return phone call by just one tiny number, and the frustration level skyrockets.

Truth to tell, most days in most businesses are rather humdrum. There are many little tasks and details to be taken care of, nothing dramatic. If you find yourself frequently frustrated and ready to scream, take that little pencil in hand and look at it for a few minutes. Then start using it as described herein. Centering on your small tasks, focusing on each piece of information, one message at a time, will reduce the frustration. All of that in a pencil! **Pencils are one of the cheapest stress management aids on the market today. And no harmful side effects if you don't swallow the lead.**

# SIX
# GOOD COMMUNICATION EQUALS LESS STRESS

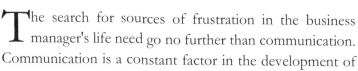

The search for sources of frustration in the business manager's life need go no further than communication. Communication is a constant factor in the development of stress-free enterprises,

The most important thing to note about communication is that messages go both ways: speaking and writing effectively are critical in management; but, so are listening and reading effectively. Everyone in the company, in addition to its customers, investors and vendors, has a stake in getting messages to the manager—and in receiving messages from the manager. The Christmas carol says this well: "Do you hear what I hear? Do you see what I see?"

The tolls caused by inaccurate messages are time lost, quality lost, and sometimes tempers going out of control. When work assignments are misunderstood, production goes wrong. When safety instructions are inaccurate, accidents happen. Orders improperly filled, inaccurately filed or sent to the wrong address lead to customer anxiety and lost business—and a bad image. If the tone of your voice is misinterpreted, or you do not pay attention to what a worker is telling you, feelings will get hurt, and loyalty may be lost.

Good communication is not a luxury, but a necessity, for business success. As a manager, you already know that your stress level will rise and fall as business success rises and falls. You also already know that poor communication is, in and of itself, very frustrating. Here are four fundamentals that come in handy as a checklist and guide for improving communication:

- **Write down relevant information,** such as phone numbers, addresses and all other information that you receive over the phone, **as you receive it.** Then read it back to check for accuracy. Yes, such a habit might add as much as one minute to every phone call. That one minute conveys to the callers that you value their messages. That habit will save you, and those who call, hundreds of hours of grief, frustration and problems every year.

- **Stay focused** by talking about one topic, and only one topic, at a time. The topic changes only after discussion of the first topic is completed. For everyone, the temptation to drift off into related topics is always there. A communication starts off about vacation schedules, but quickly becomes an account of the big fish caught last time, or the golf game coming up on the weekend—unless you insist on sticking to the first topic.

- **Listen to what you are being told.** Managers have a great deal that they need to communicate to others. It is only natural that you would feel pressured to "get your message across." But remember, those to whom you are speaking probably also have a great deal they would like to communicate to you. You, not they, are the one who is difficult to access. Their time with you is limited and valuable. So, focus on them, and let them know you are listening. You will not be heard unless you have first listened. One-way communication doesn't work very well. It also gets old in a hurry.

- **Have one conversation at a time.** Only take one phone call at a time. Only have a conversation with one person at a time when communicating face to face. Only listen to one recorded message at a time. When there are multiple conversations going on between you and other people it has become a meeting. Do not allow conversations to turn into meetings!

  It helps to look back over the day to note where was there communication-related stress:

- Was there a point when you had somebody in front

of you wanting to talk, somebody on hold and several important emails waiting for a reply?

- Did you get ambushed by several different people wanting your ear at the same time?
- Did you get customer complaints about incorrect billings?
- Did an employee or colleague complain to you that you never listen?
- Did you lose messages?
- Did you write down a wrong phone number, or accidentally delete a cell phone message?

These are the types of daily frustrations that add up to mental stress. They signal good starting points for improving communication, and providing mental peace.

As you read these simple points, you might find yourself wondering about the small and non-dramatic nature of what is being discussed. After all, isn't stress management dramatic? Nope! It is made up of small, non-dramatic and humdrum activities. It is also easy—just a matter of establishing new habits or modifying old habits. While it is for the most part humble stuff, improving in these areas is good for business and very good for you. Remember the old saying that people who listen well are known as great conversationalists!

# SEVEN
# STRESSFUL SITUATIONS: LOVE
# RELATIONSHIPS AND GRIEF

## Love Relationships at Work: A Special Kind of Stress

There will almost always be a variety of issues to be worked through and resolved in any business. Small and large businesses might have different issues, but most have issues of one sort or another that are challenging, and for which there are often no simple answers. No one wants to run a business or work in a business where policies are unsettled, and the management of the company is disorganized, hesitant or confused. These next three chapters present suggestions about typical kinds of issues that may be expected in small business management from time to time. The goal is to recognize them early, and respond appropriately. Foremost among these are love relationships in the workplace.

Love relationships at work are not anything new. People in love often want to work at the same place, so they get jobs together. Also, of course, people who work together frequently enough can fall for each other, building a love relationship that grows outside of the workplace. Sometimes these relationships are between single people, and sometimes one or both are married, making the relationship an affair. It should come as no surprise that people, whether single or married, sometimes fall in love with one another at work, just like they do in other situations of shared experiences.

It is an accepted truism among behavioral researchers that as people we are capable of falling in love any number of times during our lifetime, whether married or not. When we get close to a person who displays admirable traits, and to whom we are attracted, we react accordingly. That's the way we humans are wired. The workplace is where people generally are at their best. We dress well for work. We bring energy to work. We are diplomatic, charming, sensitive and responsive at work. We go along to get along. We accept challenges and do great things.

It is only after work, when we go home, that we dress down, run out of energy and often become rather blunt and irritable. As a whole, our nation continues to become increasingly productive with longer hours, more intense and sophisticated work, more intellect and more creativity. This requires the best that everyone has to offer. It takes focus and energy, along with brainpower and self-discipline. It demands that people be at their best while on the job. We look and act pretty good at work!

Often enough, the people at work become a team. There is a comfortable and harmonious environment. Working together builds trust. We get to know one another's strengths and weaknesses. Conflicts are kept to a minimum. There is courtesy. It is easy to like the people we work with, especially when the work environment is healthy. In such a context it is easy to develop chemistry for somebody to whom we are attracted: the "right" person. When one right person notices another right person, the chemistry kicks in. Then comes decision time: when the attraction is mutual, they have a choice. They can fan the flame, or they can pull back.

When they fan the flame, their relationship enters a new phase, one in which they are much more focused on each other. Life begins to organize around the new love. For single people, a love relationship is a life-changing experience. Generally speaking, the impact on them is very positive, and their outlook on life becomes optimistic. They are fun to be with, and their happiness radiates out to those around them—a boost for morale and a real picker-upper in the workplace.

By contrast, when one or both persons happen to be married, the choice becomes stressful: jeopardize the marriage or lose a new potential lover. Secrecy and deception only magnify the stress. The longer the new love relationship goes on, the greater the stress, and the more momentous the decision making becomes. When infidelity is a component in love relationships, there is big trouble, whatever the outcome. Love relationships, whether between single people or not, can end. The ending—whether it is simply a decision to end a budding love relationship, a decision to end an affair, or a decision to end an existing marriage or committed relationship—is a source of profound grief. Divorce brings grief and stress all its own. So, too, does breaking off a love relationship. No matter what the outcome, there will be loss, grief and stress.

We all know the variations. There can be love affairs between bosses and workers. There can be trophy wives. There can be transitional affairs or marriages, in which one or both persons marry on the rebound from the loss of a previous spouse or lover. There can be love partners who never intend to marry, and there can be same-sex love affairs. Only one thing is for certain: those involved will experience the stress that comes with trying to work things out, and/or the grief that comes with endings. The grief and tension that come with these relationships create situations in which **stress cannot be left at home because it is, in fact, generated in the workplace.**

Most workplaces are not geared toward helping with these situations. In many cases, the unwritten policy is geared toward discourage public acknowledgment. When the policy is "don't ask, don't tell," employees will find themselves in a gray area regarding job security and advancement (all the more so if you as the manager, or any others in management, are one of the parties involved). Many companies have gone down in flames because of the issues these situations set in motion. A few key points in your company policy should be in place for the purpose of guiding one and all through whatever situations might arise. If you do not have one, now would be a good time to make one, post it and ensure everyone understands it. Some points to consider in drafting such a policy:

- **A provision for counseling services, whether in the form of an Employee Assistance Program (EAP) or time off for employees to seek private counseling.**

- **A declaration that there will be no tolerance for displays of personal love relationships in the workplace.**

- **Whatever additional policy points are legally allowed, and are relevant to your company or job.**

# EIGHT
# GRIEF: HIDDEN SOURCE OF
# STRESS IN THE WORKPLACE

**The following is a personal anecdote.**

One day I was writing up findings from a research project that my partner and I were doing on the effects of ungrieved grief. The material had to do with grief about losses we feel deeply, but are ashamed to admit. Some people, for example, grieve when a pet bird or goldfish dies. They are afraid to let anyone know because, surely, to grieve for a bird is silly, isn't it? As I was working, I noticed the paper was wet. Surprised, I thought where could the wet spots be coming from?

That's when I noticed it was from the teardrops running down my cheeks! I was thinking of the prized garden our family left behind in the move from New Jersey to Oklahoma. In particular, I was crying for the tomatoes that garden produced, the largest and most productive I had ever grown. My first thought was "how ridiculous." And that was the very point of the research's findings: we grieve for anything in which we have invested ourselves, but lost. There is no such thing as "silly" grief. But because we are afraid that someone else might think our grief is silly, we assume that it is trivial and stuff it.

Stuffing grief feelings intensifies them, making the griever more angry, irritable, moody and sad. Another byproduct of grief is the feeling that nothing else, including work, is all that important by comparison. This thought can creep in and stay for a long time. It is a temptation. Grievers need to not make big decisions, at least not without talking the decisions over with others, because the sense of what is important changes so dramatically in the midst of loss.

Life is a constant series of "investments." We humans invest ourselves in people, pets, things, hobbies, interests, projects and goals. It might be a car, a boat, even a barbecue pit. It might be playing cards or tennis or gardening. It is often a significant other, children, friends or home. It can be weekends, gatherings, church or fishing. It might be a job. In fact, for a manager of a business, it very likely is that business. Life being what it is, no matter how much we love someone or something, sooner or later there will be loss. Change is inevitable. Even with good and happy events there is loss. For example:

- Weddings are happy, but the families of the new husband and wife lose a son or daughter.
- Graduations are happy, but that means a child is growing up and will leave home.
- Promotions can mean the loss of old friendships and relationships with co-workers.
- Retirement means giving up going to the office, or simply doing a meaningful job.
- Winter means no more green grass.
- Summer means no more snow skiing.

In a very real sense, there is no winning for losing. The Lord gives and the Lord takes away.

Standard workplace advice about managing stress is that work should stay at work, and home should stay at home. What makes grief a source of stress at work is that grief does not stay home. When we grieve, we bring our grief with us. Our feelings go where we go. To stuff the grief is to be stressed. When the loss involves a person at work, the stress is all the greater, just as when the loss involves a person at home, it is difficult to escape the reminders of grief. Among the many variations of grief common within the business environment are:

- Ending a love relationship with a coworker.
- Anticipatory grief over an approaching retirement or promotion.
- Losing a friend who gets transferred, promoted or

fired; losing an office; changing

- Responsibilities or ending a project that was particularly satisfying.

The next time you wonder what it is that is actually bothering one of your team members—perhaps a once highly efficient, cheerful worker has suddenly changed—ask about loss and grief. Listen closely. The next time you get feedback from those with whom you work that you, not they, are the one who is out of sorts, do a little inventory of what you have lost, or are losing.

Everyone is grumpy or moody for a reason. It's just that sometimes we are not aware of—or are ashamed to share—what is really going on inside of ourselves. The grieving person is building up powerful emotional steam, especially anger. Confrontation, while never advisable in the workplace, is especially harmful in the grieving context, whether it is your grief, or that of somebody you supervise.

Managing a business often means working with difficult people, and people who are having difficulties. Explore appropriate management approaches designed to take into account an employee's need for grief support, while at the same time maintaining good business practices. One size will not fit all. Grief support is a key factor in employee retention, deserving of careful thought and attention. What should you do?

- Be a good listener. But remember, your job as a manager is to listen, not to counsel or conduct therapy.

- Consider providing a room or private area were workers can grieve, as needed, for a few minutes, while regaining self-control.
- Grant work leave for grief counseling appointments.
- Keep touch with the grieving person until they are mending, tailoring their responsibilities to accommodate their need to grieve.
- Bear in mind: grief is a process of healing, not a disease or sickness. Your biggest help as a manager will be patience and support. In the case of your own grief, accept support
- From those around you to whatever extent practical, and consider getting
- Professional help outside of your work environment, whether that be an office or home-based work site.

**Time does not heal all wounds, only clean wounds. The way to clean grief wounds is with tears. Let them flow.**

# NINE
# BURNOUT

## Physiology of the Stress Reaction

The reaction to stressors begins with perception. We see, foresee or experience threats or significant changes in our situation, and the brain interprets this as danger. Our bodies immediately go into fight-or-flight mode. Adrenaline floods through us, the eyes become alert and active, hearing sharpens, the heart rate increases, blood pressure goes up and the digestive system closes down. We focus on the danger to the point that other things go unnoticed.

In most cases there is no fight to resolve the situation, and flight is impossible. There is no escaping financial problems, illness, bad news, a tense work situation, grief or relationship conflicts. Our bodies remain on a heightened state of alert, still prepared to fight or flee, with periodic increases and decreases of intensity. Within a few days, the reaction for most people becomes "normal," and we put it down as "having a worry." This is a signal that the stressor now appears as a given on our mental screen.

Each time we focus on that given in our mind, the stress reaction happens. The brain does not register the difference between a real danger and a mentally perceived danger, so the reaction to a "worry" is the same as if the event were actually happening. That is why we cry, get angry or become tense when watching movies. Since the body is not intended to be in the fight/flight mode for more than a few hours at any given time, stress creates changes in appetite, mood swings, energy swings, fatigue, a vague sense of unease and periods of hyperactivity or depression. We begin to crave relief and escape.

Keeping to a schedule becomes more problematic. We skip meals, have trouble sleeping or go off our regular sleep schedule. We overdo things, and/or skip chores or tasks. Life begins to pile up, and we sometimes feel overwhelmed. We become more difficult to both live and work with. It takes effort to be calm yet alert, to focus on the tasks at hand and make good decisions. Little tasks seem big, and minor irritations seem major. People begin to get on our nerves. **We have become stressed!**

**Stress happens not because of events, or the possibility that terrible events will happen, but because of our reaction to events and likelihoods.**

## Burnout

The word "burnout" is a buzzword. It is used, loosely, to mean that persons have experienced enough pressure and anxiety (stress) over a long enough period of time to finally make them throw in the towel. The stress can be at work, in which case they give up their job or career. Or the stress can be with their family, spouse or significant other, in which case they end the relationship or run away from home. In a somewhat related usage, people also speak of becoming burned out on hobbies, sports, volunteer work or other focused activities; but what they usually mean is simply that they have become bored, feel a lack of challenge, have lost enthusiasm and need to give it a rest, whatever "it" happens to be.

Work-related burnout is a common phenomenon across our industrialized world. For the most part it is completely preventable. If you know what to watch for, there are things you can do to prevent your own burnout, and that of the people you supervise. **In a nutshell, burnout is what happens when stress gets out of hand for a long period of time. It is the disaster waiting to happen when stress management practices are ignored.** It makes little difference whether you are the person in charge as a one-person business, a business owner, a business manager or just simply "the boss." As the

leader, there are stress management practices that make a difference and which, when practiced, head off burnout and lead to a more peaceful, enjoyable and long-lasting workplace environment. At that point, you become the hero!

Stress in the workplace is not news. Every increase in productivity comes about not by magic, but by effort and intensity. The workforce pulls together, works hard, puts in long hours and concentrates. The standards are set high. Of course there is stress! Stress can lead to the loss of the highest motivated workers, managers and executives when it becomes burnout. One would think that the highest motivated people, especially among the ranks of managers and executives, would be the ones with the most staying power. But stress allowed to run out of control is not respectful of rank: nobody is immune.

## There are five types of burnout:

- leave the business or profession forever
- above it all
- trapped in a gilded cage
- dead wood
- helpless and hopeless

## Burnout Type One: Leave the Business or Profession Forever

The most highly motivated people are often in the type of work they love. They are easy to spot when they interview for a position: they are the ones who always wanted to be a teacher, minister, doctor, nurse, computer whiz, laboratory manager, researcher, coach, programmer, scientist, engineer or any of the hundreds of other possible types of career/work identity in today's world. They read books and watched movies that portrayed what they dreamed of becoming. They worked hard at school. They went to college or technical school to achieve a foundation for what they planned on doing for the rest of their life.

These people hit the ground running when they are hired. They come in early, stay late, work during breaks, ask questions and emote enthusiasm. Sometimes they give union stewards a headache because they set the bar so high. They are not necessarily popular with coworkers or co-managers for the same reason. They may be respected but also resented. If you put them in charge of company events, they will push, pull and prod everyone else into doing their part and more. These are the mechanics who take the manuals home to study in their spare time, the teachers who come back on weekends to make their classrooms and labs more learning efficient and those who tell you that their job is a dream come true.

Those heading for this type of burnout know no restraint, and cannot pace themselves. They are like a plane going full throttle all the time. In the beginning, they usually get encouraged by whoever is in charge, or by the success of their business. Eventually, they get feedback about pacing themselves, slowing down, giving it a rest, thinking about the long haul. Those who hear this good advice and take it to heart do well over the long haul, and do not burn out. Those who ignore it mistake the advice as temptation to become mediocre. They misread and misinterpret the hints to slow down as leading to laziness, lack of commitment or downright selfishness They have embarked on the burnout path that ends with leaving the business or profession forever.

The journey is swift and often ends abruptly. Like a flaming meteor, they crash, exhausted and disillusioned. The very ideals that brought them to their dreamed-of-work become the reasons for which they leave. The explosion might be a tirade against the company, industry or coworkers. The bitterness may be over feeling unappreciated or used. The conviction might be that the whole operation has lost its vision and commitment. It might simply be profound discouragement or exhaustion. This burned out person leaves forever, often turning on the very people at the top who, at first, were thrilled to have such a motivated person on board. The operation loses one of its most valuable people. Others look on and scratch their heads in bewilderment.

Such tragedies are easily avoided with a few sound practices revolving around supervision, mentoring, leadership and self-pacing. These are the "racehorses" who should be encouraged and taught how to pace themselves. Their zeal should be tempered, not encouraged. They should be paired with experienced people, who can mentor them to match their pace, instead of trying to outrun everybody around them. They should not be allowed to skip vacations. They need to leave work at work, and quit at quitting time. When they are sick, they need to take sick leave. When they volunteer for extra duty, they should be thanked but refused.

If the description of this type of burnout happens to fit you, do two things immediately in order to head it off. First, **take some vacation time and get as far away as practical** for at least a few days. Second, **find a reliable, trusted person to talk to about this, and do so by the hour. Such a person may be a life coach, a professional counselor or therapist, a trusted friend who respects confidentiality, a business advisor. Do NOT turn to a romantic relationship for the answer, and do not use or abuse any substances, legal or illegal, for relief.** The first objective is to regain perspective, whether that means guiding a worker, or taking care of yourself.

## Burnout Type 2: Above It All

Workplace stress will run its course if left unchecked. The end result, for those who continue working in this condition, is frequently figuring out a way to get "above it all." The person has become allergic to whatever their job entails. He or she probably did their job well for a very long time, perhaps with little or no challenge. The job could be anything from an accounting function to a hands-on repetitive manual labor function. It could be teaching, counseling, social work, being a prison guard, or running a drill press. Nearly any job, at any level, in any type of business or profession, can become the source of burnout for the person who does the same repetitive work. The person decides that if they never do the function again, it will be too soon. But they cannot leave for whatever reason. And so what happens? **They get promoted!**

This is the supervisor who raves about the good memories of working on the assembly line before getting promoted. But you will never see that supervisor in work clothes again. He or she will never again get anywhere near the assembly line. This is the education administrator who gives speeches about the joy of teaching, but will never again set foot in a classroom—the one who loves students, but hasn't even tutored or substitute taught in years, and who never will in the future. This form of burnout serves two purposes. First, it allows persons to go on working at a higher level in a new position. Secondly, it insulates them from something they never want to do again, with the added bonus that no one will ever know their secret.

The danger to the company or organization with this person is that, in fact, they rarely make good executives because the promotion is simply serving the purpose of insulating them from a function at which they burned out. They have been promoted beyond their level of competence. The hope would be that the promotion serves as a new beginning, and that enough lessons were learned so as to avoid flaming out in the new position.

## What Are Those Lessons?

**First and foremost, challenge and variety** are important in any job. Ignore that need and stress builds, partly through boredom, and partly through revulsion. It is human nature to be repulsed by what has become burdensome to the point of intolerance. **Second, honest praise and feedback** to the worker in repetitive functions helps to underline the importance and significance of the function. Everyone needs that reminder, especially when the job can manifest a feeling of drudgery.

## Additional stress breakers:

- Frequent work breaks.
- Developing non-job related interests and challenges when not at work.
- Developing more job skills and achieving advancement as a result.

Ignore these steps, and what rises to the top will not be cream, but instead will be numbed-out human debris disguised as management material. This is not fair to the person or the company or the organization. Promotion becomes escape. On the other hand, imagine yourself promoting these steps with those whose work you supervise. Commit to developing and supporting a cheerful workplace environment by encouraging and supporting all the people who do the work. Give yourself some pats on the back.

## What If You Got Promoted in Order to Be Above It All?

If you sought a promotion so that you could avoid doing a job that was burning you out, use your promotion to begin a different approach to work. Learn to learn. Accept challenges. Think again about how you experience stress, and explore new strategies for tending to your stress. Force yourself to contribute in some meaningful manner to your company and fellow workers. Seek counseling or coaching that allows you to talk it out with a good listener who is knowledgeable about these matters.

## Burnout Type #3: Trapped in a Gilded Cage

We have all met them: the highly successful businessperson, the indispensable boss, the key team member. They are the best at what they do. They are appreciated by everyone. They are making money hand over fist. They have high blood pressure and heart problems. They drive a nice car. They live in a nice house. They often have a wonderful family or trophy wife. They are at the top of their game, and could drop dead at any moment. They are usually well mannered, sometimes charming. They smile and laugh. But what you see is all you get. They are not happy. They are trapped. The bars of their cage are made of gold. Our culture makes it difficult to believe that success can be stressful. We are taught that lack of success is stressful. If only we could make it to the top, everything would fall into place. We would be happy, and those we love would be secure. Our worries would be over. The kingdom would come.

Such behavior is often called "Type A Behavior," and it comes with a price. Most of the time, success requires a very large amount of dedication, energy and focus. Those who get to the top of the mountain say that it is a difficult climb, with many sacrifices, such as sleep deprivation, lack of pastimes, little (if any) leisure time and a great deal of focused intensity. These days, the formula also includes physical workouts and careful attention to nutrition.

## So, What Is the Stress of Success All About?

Simple answer: the plan is working, but not yet

accomplished. The successful person has gotten halfway across the bridge, far enough out so that there is no turning back, but not yet to the other side; and he or she lacks the energy or resources to make it the rest of the way. It is the point of "do or die." Often the problem is financial: too much debt to afford retirement, too many payments to cut back on work (but not enough stamina to keep up the pace). This person has become all work and no play. The doctor worries about this person's prognosis at bedside, saying the choice is to cut back, or have a more serious heart attack or stroke.

American business is loaded with people heading for this type of burnout. They are to be found at every level, from lowest level worker to top executive, and everywhere in between. In big business firms, the corporate culture rewards success. In the 23 million small businesses, the name of the game is produce or perish. Time has become money. So, stress management begins by recognizing that success brings stress. There truly is stress that does need to be managed or eliminated. Physical workouts and proper nutrition are part of the program. Other parts of the program need to include:

- time-outs.
- proper amounts of rest and sleep.
- relaxation.
- effective venting of tension.
- setting limits.

Setting limits is probably the greatest challenge of all.

Those successful people who learn to set limits are likely to live long enough to enjoy their success. Those who do not set realistic limits will likely succeed as well. Their obituaries will note that they died at the very pinnacle of their success.

Tragedy, in the view of Greek philosophy, was suffering that did not need to happen. Some bad things happen in life, and cannot be avoided. But other bad things happen because we did not have the wisdom to avoid them. Success does not need to be overly stressful (and certainly not "overly successful"). It is possible to have your cake and eat it too. But one needs to learn stress management. Build into the plan for success clear provisions for being human.

**Being successful does not end being human. Humans need to manage their stress, and avoid unnecessary stress. Successful people need to manage the stress of success.**

What if you are the one trapped in a gilded cage? First, remember that you have a lot going for you to have gotten this far! Rather than isolate in your stress, seek out a trustworthy person with whom to talk, until you are able to regain perspective. It's almost never an either/or situation, but it usually feels that way: do or die, with no middle ground between success and failure. Clearly, there needs to be an adjustment to the plan, not an end to the plan! But "clear" is not easy to come by when in the throes of burnout. Find that trustworthy friend, that professional counselor, that listening ear, that person who has experienced what you are experiencing and learned from it. Then let that person help you learn from your experience, before changing your plan. Attorneys point out that it is better to consult before making a mistake, than afterwards. How true!

## Burnout Types #4 and #5: Dead Wood and Helpless/Hopeless

When stress beats people down long enough, the fight goes out of them. The job must be endured to the bitter end. The end is retirement. And so, when the worker burns out, the strategy becomes one of hiding from the limelight (dead wood), or going into a helpless/hopeless mode that forces management to perform a rescue, or make a decision for the worker.

The "**dead wood**" burned out person becomes highly skilled at achieving invisibility. They never volunteer. They keep quiet at meetings, do not argue, ensure they are not noticed and, in the case of votes, always vote the right way by making sure which way the wind is blowing. The goal of achieving and contributing in the workplace changes to a new goal of hanging around until retirement, keeping the paychecks coming, not getting fired. Taking no chances becomes the way of life.

The **helpless and hopeless"** burned out person needs help all the time, is also afraid to take any chances and requires constant supervision. Their work quantity and quality is minimal, and they are incapable of initiative. Their slogan is "don't blame me, I'm doing the best I can." This person uses sick leave frequently and has a hard time making ends meet. Life at work becomes overwhelming. Sometimes life at home has also become overwhelming. They are victims in their own minds.

Both of these forms of burnout are preventable. Once they set in, however, the challenge of remedying the situation is significant. There needs to be a personal plan, mutually agreed upon by the worker and the supervisor, tailored to the needs of both the worker and company or organization. There needs to be support and encouragement. But how much help is appropriate? A buyout or termination may become the only truly viable options.

Dead wood and helpless/hopeless employees are a blemish on any company's top management. This form of burnout is something that should never happen with proper supervision and management. Workplace stress should be noted and addressed long before it comes to the point of burnout. That is one more reason why, from time to time, executives do well to consider coaching, consultations or training for their management personnel and themselves. The outsider looking in can sometimes notice things at a glance which are not obvious to those on the inside, making suggestions that can amount to that one extra ounce of prevention.

Managers, talk to your employees. Listen to what they say about their work, their aspirations, their frustrations and their future. Do this with everybody, but even more so with the dead wood and hopeless/helpless person. Help this person to make a new plan. **Believe in their ability to the point that they, too, regain belief in their ability.**

# TEN
# FAMILY OWNED BUSINESSES
# A TALE OF TWO BROTHERS

## Bill Smith

Bill Smith inherited Smith Oil. His father had developed a small cluster of high-producing oil wells, built a small refinery and recruited other well owners in the region to use the refinery. When Bill took over the business, he built service stations in a 100-mile radius from the refinery. He used his own gasoline, refined from his wells, added fuel retail operations to the core business and then added fast food and convenience store items to the retail operations. He placed the entire business into a family trust that included his wife and children, along with his brothers, sisters and his wife's siblings. All told, there were, by the time he reached his prime, nine families with 36 individuals drawing funds from the trust each year.

Bill was very busy and very popular. His light brown hair and blue eyes complemented his almost constant smile. His approach was to make work and family life one and the same. That way, he reasoned, he could be in contact with family even while on the job. He wouldn't need to stop work at quitting time to go home and be with family if he hired family members into the business. He hired his wife and son into the operation. Over time, he also hired a brother and sister-in-law, and would bring on various other family members with each passing year. He did this not because they had any special qualifications in well head management, refinery operations, management, exploration, accounting or retailing, but because he simply wanted family to be working with him in the business. That was the reason. He wanted all the family members to share in the wealth. After all, there would be plenty more oil. He would expand the operation by drilling new wells, and by buying up leases on already producing wells.

The plan went very well for a few years because Bill worked around the clock. He looked after wells, maintained tanker trucks, conferred every day with his refinery boss and made the rounds to his retail outlet managers. Work was his life—seven days a week, 52 weeks per year, sunrise to sunset. When he went home, he took work with him. The logs, records, production numbers and tax reports were endless. Soon his office at home spilled over into other parts of their home. Pictures of the wells, fuel stops, trucks and employees began to appear on the walls. Business records began to fill up their shelves and closets. File cabinets began to replace furniture. Computers in several rooms were dedicated to various aspects of the business. Conversations at home were almost always about business. Bill's wife, predictably, soon became sick of hearing about the price fluctuations per barrel of oil and cubic foot of natural gas. Family get-togethers became smaller and less frequent, as one and all began to dread being around Bill, and the constant conversation about business and industry issues. For some family and many friends, Bill was the boss. People felt increasingly awkward being with the boss when off duty, especially when it appeared that the boss was never truly off duty.

Bill's next mistake was predictable: he ignored his doctor's advice. High blood pressure and anxiety were the diagnoses. The doc wanted Bill to start exercising, set a firm quitting time on weekdays and take the weekends off. Bill considered this advice to be impossible. He had taken the company so far, and borrowed so much money to expand and build market territory, that there could be no slowing down at this time. The whole operation was so successful, too successful to throttle back. In just a few more years he would have the right people in place, debts paid down and the time to retire, with the family trust secured.

**He was trapped in a golden cage: too successful to retrench, but not quite to the goal. Besides, there were so many people depending on him, both for their jobs,**

**and income from the trust.**

With the smile gone, the twinkle in the eye fading and the hair turned gray, it took his first heart attack to convince Bill that he was killing himself with success. Soon after, the divorce got him thinking about the purpose of life, especially his own.

## Rob

Rob, one of Bill's brothers, had worked briefly at the family business that Bill was expanding. After eight months, Rob realized that there was nothing about oil wells, natural gas, refinery operation or fuel retailing that he would ever like. He knew the stress would be great, and the satisfaction minimal. He and his wife decided that there is more to life than working, especially working at something they did not like. They spent time thinking about what they enjoyed. She loved flowers, and he liked gardening. So, she began studying the flower industry, while he took classes in organic farming. Together they opened a small specialty business, utilizing a few acres of land and a greenhouse. They slowly built a clientele, selling flowers and organic vegetables. They worked together at their business, kept studying, and little-by-little, enlarged the operation to the point where it supported them.

They quit at quitting time most days. They took Sundays off, and went on short getaway vacations three or four times every year. They pledged not to discuss business after hours, and kept that pledge. During spring and summer, peak season for weddings flowers, they hired part-time help. They also hired part-time workers for help with their organically grown fruits and vegetables during the Thanksgiving-to-Christmas holidays. They only hired qualified, hard-working persons. Many of their part-time workers came back year after year. Some of them began taking classes to learn more about what they were doing.

**Best of all, Rob's doctor told him after his last physical that he had the body of a nineteen-year-old, and a heart that could last another 25 years!**

## Why the Contrast?

All of us have made the kinds of mistakes Bill made, or have known people who did. The variations are many. Not all the people who own and manage their new businesses have the training and experience necessary when they get started. We learn by experience—if we allow ourselves to learn. The prevailing work ethic is to work until we drop, then work some more! Of course, this "good old American way" is not good for business, and it is not a good way to manage stress. Look back at how Bill could have done it differently:

- He could have run the family business like a business, only hiring family members if they were qualified and needed.
- He could have limited his work to working hours, and left it at the office.
- As the business expanded, he should not have expanded the amount of time he gave to it, but instead hired and trained people to grow with the

expansion.

Bill assumed that family life and business could be intertwined in a beneficial manner. They usually cannot be intertwined with good results. He also neglected to develop a life for his wife and himself, his children or his extended family. He was all business, making himself a dull boy.

Bill opened his business life while still getting ready to have a life, only to be struck down because of the very success he worked so hard to achieve. Stress does not know delay. It will take its toll, no matter what plans we have to outlast or ignore it. This tale of two brothers is the tale of everyone who owns or runs a family business or businesses. The moral of the story is always the same.

**Run the family business like a business, not like a family.**

# ELEVEN
# STRESS PREVENTION IN FAMILY-OWNED BUSINESSES

Family-owned businesses present golden opportunities for family feuds. As the business manager, you have an extra challenge: run the business well, while also serving the interests of the family. Disagreements about the business present a frequent and serious challenge for all concerned. It is your responsibility to make sure these disagreements are taken seriously and resolved, for the sake of both the business, and the family that owns the business. Many marriages and families have been destroyed by quarrels over the family-owned business; and many businesses have been destroyed for the same reason.

Attorneys, counselors and advisors typically take note of not only who owns the business—and how the ownership is structured—but how the family will relate to the business. On a somber note, for example, they will encourage the family to protect the business against divorce, death and inheritance taxes. As painful as that might be, it is better to address these issues at the beginning of the business, well before any tragic events occur. You may need to insist on getting these issues decided—not fun, but certainly necessary.

Protecting the business against daily meddling by family members also falls to you, as the business manager. It is your responsibility to defend your turf. You, not family members, do the managing. **Bring to bear sound business practices, articulate them frequently and defend them always.** Remember, at the root of all too many eternal family quarrels and feuds, are disagreements over three questions. Even when family members intervene, getting themselves hired into the business, the issues will still boil down to these three questions:

- who should be in charge?
- is the wealth being justly distributed?
- is the business being properly managed?

## Who is Responsible for What?

Sound business practice begins with making sure everyone involved agrees to their responsibilities. The Board makes policy. The manager operates the business according to the policies laid down by the Board. The executive group of the Board provides day-to-day support for the manager, oversees the implementation of policy and acts as a buffer between the rest of the owners and the manager. The owners are responsible for making sure there is a Board, and that the Board develops policy that is in line with the wishes of the owners, as well as the demands of sound business principles. When family members or other owners come to you to discuss policy changes, refer them to the Board. Be careful about giving your opinions about policy to anyone except the Board, and any family members and/or other owners, as directed by the Board.

To those who ask whether it is best to have a non-family member manage the family-owned business, I contend that it does not matter. What matters is that the manager be well-suited to the job. If the manager is to be a family member, he or she still needs to observe the professional guidelines of managing, and not take sides or participate in any family disagreements about the business. That is to say, do not wear two hats. Involvement by the manager in family politics will be the kiss of death, for the business and for the family.

## About Those Three Questions:

- The Board should be in charge of policy. The manager should be in charge of running the business.

- Whether the wealth is being justly distributed is for the family and Board to decide.

- Whether the business is being properly manage is for you, as the manager, and the Board to decide.

Family-owned businesses that do not have a Board and executive group are well advised to get them in place, and start using them. Do not allow yourself, as the manager, to be substituted for the Board or executive group. Make sure to develop a Board that operates well and acts like a Board, not existing simply as a formality. The Board needs to work hard at developing and evaluating policy, making policy changes when needed. The executive group of the Board can consist of several Board members. Their role is to assist and support the manager, while occasionally making policy recommendations to the Board.

## Use the Structure

Once the company structure is in place, use it to keep family-generated stress out of the business. The answer when a family member wants to be hired by you for a position that is open? "Yes," if that person is qualified, and company policy allows it. "No," if that person is not qualified, or company policy does not allow it. The same goes for all other interactions between you, as the manager (whether or not you are a family member), and members of the family. Requests for loans from the company to a family member? Same answer: look to the policy. Help the Board make good policy. Then stick to that policy. That is what it takes for family-owned businesses to be free of interference. Apply this approach to your family-owned business, and enjoy the peace. **Run the business like a business, not like a family. Policy is the manager's best friend.**

## Run the Business Like a Business

"Family business" means many things to many people, from the family farm, to the heirs who own or run business empires built by their ancestors, and millions of small businesses in between.

These might be a husband-wife or parent-child team. It might be family members developing former farmland into a nursery, or managing their golf course. It might be siblings-turned-partners trying their hand at a new business. It might be relatives working for relatives. The variations are endless because families are unique. The opportunities for family-owned-and-run business come in many sizes and shapes, from one-person businesses to empires.

As the manager of a family business, you can utilize principles gleaned from the experience of others, who have walked in your shoes. Much of that experience was painful. Managing family businesses is "tricky." Your stress level will be lower, much lower, if you learn from the experience of others. Here are four of those lessons.

1. **Base business decisions on business issues** such as the market, product/service demand, inventory issues, costs, cash flow, competition and the like. Do not base decisions on whose feelings might get hurt, whose loyalties could be betrayed or what old scores haven't been settled. Family members in a family business are challenged to put aside family dynamics in favor of business principles, and business-like behaviors. Sometimes adult children need to

supervise their parents. Sometimes a family member needs to be the boss (manager) even though he or she is neither the oldest, smartest or most respected member of the family. Sometimes the family needs to hire an outside person to be the manager.

2. **Be Guided by the Business Plan and Company Policies.** Be sure to have a business plan—and stick to it! A business plan will separate business from personal considerations. The manager is simply following the plan. Unpopular decisions are not personal! The mere fact that you manage according to the plan (and Board policies) serves to emphasize that the business is business, no matter how many family members might be involved.

3. **Debate the Business Plan Only at Scheduled Intervals.** Families value peace and stability. Once family decisions are made, there is little desire to consider change and start debating all over again, much less risk triggering new arguments. Business, however, is not like that. There must be an openness to change, particularly in light of changing factors, such as competition, market trends, labor and production costs.

4. **Consider the success factor.** Business success means growth, and a subsequent need to carefully consider the best uses of increased funds from cash flow, methods for sheltering profits from taxes and ways to handle surplus funds. Sometimes, family members are tempted to view company profits as their piggy bank. The manager must take

responsibility to prevent raids on the piggy bank, if the business is to endure.

5. **Be Sure to Seek Appropriate Professional Advice.** Whether it be accounting, legal, marketing or tax matters, keep informed; and be sure you are guided by the best current thinking. Remember, the tendency in families is to set a course, and stick with it. Decisions made in the past might not fit today's trends. To the extent that you report to the Board advice from professionals, you are giving a second message, as well: opinions based on family considerations must be considered differently than professional business advice.

In families, the views of each member matter, and should be considered. The goal is to promote good relationships and mutual support (positive alliances and cohesion). In business, the goal is to succeed with the business. **Family members are challenged to be good employees, good workers, good business directors, good owners and good business team players, while putting aside personal matters.** Separating family from business opinions and decisions is neither easy nor totally achievable, but it should be the goal. If you do separate them, you will have far fewer nightmares—awake or asleep!

**Like all businesses, family businesses vary greatly.**

**Stick with sound business practices.**

**Separate personal matters from business matters.**

**Follow a sound, well-informed business plan.**

Take good advice, and change when change is merited.

## Be Prepared for Success

The "stress of success" sounds like a contradiction. After all, aren't we supposed to be relieved and joyful when we succeed? But it is not ridiculous to be stressed by success. For anyone managing a small business, the phrase applies. In particular, the manager of a business that has grown from one person to many employees, or blossomed into a larger endeavor, will likely experience the peculiar stress that comes with succeeding. Success brings with it profound transitions in how the owners and managers are perceived. Often the perceptions are over-inflated and under-informed by persons not directly associated with the business. The business also gets targeted as a potential customer for a variety of enterprise services and products. This creates considerable stress, and should be taken seriously. Consider what happens when a small business "takes off" and becomes well-known.

## Fame

Your neighbors and friends know about you. It is assumed that you are successful as a result of getting all the breaks, knowing the right people, stealing and cheating, selling drugs out the back door, inheriting money, playing the angles. Overnight you have gone from being a hard working neighbor to some kind of slick operator—in the minds of some people.

## Visibility

The ad in your local phone book or newspaper means you are no longer anonymous. customers know your address and phone number. There is nowhere to hide! You have become a big-shot!

## Wealth

The whole world seems to think you are rich. You are now expected to respond to requests for sponsorship of every good cause known to mankind. Why aren't you interested in helping the local brotherhoods and orders of police, firefighters and first responders; starving people, auxiliaries, and churches; and the United Way, Jerry's Kids, UNESCO and zillions of other charities? Don't you care?

## Needy

You are assumed to need, desperately, immediate help to make your business more successful. Why aren't you ordering all the business advice magazines designed just for you? Why aren't you joining all the business organizations out there dedicated to speaking for your interests? Why aren't you going to the conventions, renting exhibit booths and hiring consulting firms? Why aren't you signing up with investment funds that will multiply your great profits by the day? Every bank on earth wishes to lend you money, especially with business credit cards and home equity loans. The more business you do, the more solicitations you will receive. You are successful, after all, so start borrowing. Of course, if you really need the money…never mind.

## Insurance

Several dozen insurance companies will think your situation is just right for their products. These might be health insurance; long-term health care; life, accident, home or auto insurance; flood, liability or credit care insurance or any combination of similar products. The truth dawns: if you are in business, and have been successful enough to get noticed, you will spend the rest of your life hearing about insurance.

So, successful businessperson that you are, in charge of a successful and growing small company, get with the program. Admit it! You are rich, slick, a borderline criminal, in need of help from all directions to become richer. And you are stingy if you do not contribute generously to all causes. You should be out there in the community providing leadership in every moment of spare time. You should be happy to receive mail by the pound. You should be a pillar of the church, and a model for all. You should join organizations. You should spend hours reading business advice columns after you finish devouring the Wall Street Journal every day.

## Bottom Line

The bottom line of this discussion of "success" is to make two points. **First**, the transition from small business to larger business, or from one-person operation to multi-employee enterprise, is taken as success, changing how you are perceived. You can expect to become the target of marketing and solicitation. You can expect to be perceived as wealthy, powerful and influential. You are still the same person, but it may seem like no one else believes that. It can be very confusing and stressful. Keep your eye on the ball: developing a business is hard work. When utilizing your time and energy, your first priority is your business, not anyone else's cause, business propositions or perceptions of what you should be doing.

**Secondly,** two of the easiest and quickest ways to manage the stress of success are humor, and communication. So, make the jokes and exaggerate. Keep saying that all the praise and admiration are something you appreciate, but cannot take too seriously. Listen for feedback from anybody who will truly understand what you are saying and experiencing. Ignore the rest.

**Success changes very little in terms of the daily running of the business, but it greatly changes the perceptions of all those onlookers. Do not get carried away by accolades and laurels. You are the same person, and it is the same business, before and after the applause.**

# TWELVE
# WORKING AT HOME AND WORK
# PHILOSOPHY

At first blush, one might suppose home-based businesses, and working at home for somebody else, would be stress free. After all, look at the advantages: you are your own boss, make your own schedule, work when you feel like it and have no traffic jams to and from the office! But look more closely, considering the following factors.

## Your Own Boss

Being the boss means that now you, not somebody else, must take responsibility for all the tasks related to managing the business. These include checking for regulatory compliance, tax reporting, maintaining business checking accounts, planning and managing inventory, order taking, accounting (keeping the books), advertising, marketing, delivery, billing and reading the mail. It's not that any one of these (or dozens of other) tasks are necessarily complicated. Some of them, in fact, might be boring, such as sifting through the junk mail to make sure you don't miss an important letter or bill.

If you work at home, but are working for some other business (distance employee), you are STILL the manager, in that you must manage your time, phone calls, mail, reports, filing and so forth. What can be stressful is the multiplicity of tasks. Put another way, being your own boss means keeping track of unending and unrelenting details. There needs to be a quick, efficient system for getting all these details out of the way in order to do the actual business. That's where the stress develops. It is up to you to make sure that no time is wasted brooding over bills, mail is not piling up, there is no delay in filing or storing of data, and that there is no time wasted trying to decide what to save, and what to throw away.

Then there are those unending phone calls to be dealt with. "The boss" does everything, that's the job description, whether you work at home for your business or someone else's. Whether the task is secretarial or executive in nature, the at-home manager does it—and the pressure is to do it right now. Get behind in a home-based business, and there will be instant stress; because getting behind means that tomorrow there will be twice as much to do as there was today. The art to be developed here is **multi-tasking.** Know how much multi-tasking you can do, and stay within those limits.

## Your Own Schedule

Working at home is only possible when you are working at home! The problem with being at home is that there are other things to be done that do not relate to the business:

- preparing and eating meals
- keeping the house orderly and clean
- answering the doorbell
- setting out the trash
- taking care of any dependents
- feeding the pets
- bringing in the paper and the mail
- visiting with the neighbors
- helping with rides, laundry, errands and other chores
- entertaining and obligatory social duties

Unless one is living absolutely alone in a perfectly managed apartment or condo, it is nearly impossible to be home without having "life" get in the way. Once you have made a work schedule, that real stress begins: keeping to the schedule, instead of doing the things that need doing for home maintenance and daily living. Sticking to the schedule means no TV interruptions, no extended phone conversations, no time-outs to run up to the store or take a quick siesta! Working alone is often boring, tiring and non-stimulating. There is no companionship or joking around, no other workers to pick up the slack, or form a team approach. You do it, or it does not get done. You work no matter what mood you are in, and no matter how you are feeling physically. Anytime you break with the schedule, the business stops, and work piles up.

The art to be developed here is **focus and concentration.** Some might describe it as self-discipline. Focusing is a mental activity. It is helpful to make a work schedule that takes account of your ability to focus, and reflects the limits you have regarding how long you are able to concentrate at any one time.

## The Myth of Working When You Feel Like Working

This myth is the downfall of many a business or at-home job! Working only when we feel like working is what describes a hobby, not a business. For those who only work when they feel like working, hobbies are the better choice. The art to be developed here is **determination and perseverance.** Any other approach will be a stress producer, and will be difficult to sustain.

## No Commuting

Despite the complaining, commuting is not all bad. It gives drivers and passengers a good separation time between work and home, something essential for reducing stress at both work and home. This be a time for listening to the news or to music. It might be conversation with others. It might just be time for concentrating on the traffic situation. Traffic jams are like feeding pigeons: they get our minds off what we are leaving, before we engage with what will be happening at our destination. By working at home and not commuting, the transition from workplace to home is gone. The challenge becomes separating your workplace at home from your living space at home: making sure your office area is well defined, and used only for work. Do not take any of your work materials from that office into the rest of your home. Set a work schedule for yourself. When your workday is finished, close up your work, shut the office and stay out of it. Do not let work and life intermingle. By closing down your work and workspace, you will have an easier time shutting down your mind to business, and opening it to your life.

## Avoid Interruptions

Unless you are living alone, you will also need to prevent work interruptions by others who live with you. Request that they not intrude into your workspace during your work hours. Make sure everyone knows when those hours begin and end. If necessary, post your hours! While it may be impossible to prevent all interruptions, it is always possible to keep them at a minimum; but that will only happen if you make it happen. If you want it to happen, you will make it happen. Explain to those with whom you live why it needs to happen. Coordinate your schedules until everybody gets on board with the notion that work life, and the rest of life, are best separated in order to avoid or minimize work stress.

## Work Philosophy

Working at home is, for many people, a trigger for

reflecting about why we work in the first place. What's the point? For what? There are, in fact, only so many answers. Some people work in order to pay for what they really want out of their life. They endure work so that they can afford to go fishing or hunting, or have a ski vacation every year; build that home by the seashore, or in the mountains or woods; or enjoy a hobby. Work is mostly a necessary evil.

Others work because work gives their life meaning and purpose: work is their life. Time out from work is mostly for the purpose of resting up so as to resume the work that they do so well. Work is a blessing, its own reward.

For most of us, work is probably somewhere in the middle, meaningful, but also a means to an end. But for all of us, no matter what work means, what we do or where we do it, stress is always a key factor to be considered. Stress is never good for us. For the most part, stress can be eliminated, avoided, or greatly reduced. It is my hope for you, the reader, that your work will be less stressful, and more enjoyable, as you use as many of the principles described in this book as are practical in your situation. Be happy in your work? That's an option. Be stress free in your work? That's a goal worth pursuing. God bless you in your work.

# Recommended Reading:

**Conflict at Work by** Dr. M Paula Daoust

**Turn Around Trauma by** Dr. Richard K. Nongard

**The Secrets to Healthy Self-Esteem** by Alfred Bellanti

**Be You to Be Full** by Connie Jo Holmes

Made in the USA
Columbia, SC
09 February 2021

32615702R00059